Inuit Art

Cape Dorset

Address Book

Pomegranate

SAN FRANCISCO

Published by Pomegranate Communications, Inc.
Box 808022, Petaluma CA 94975
800-227-1428; www.pomegranate.com

Pomegranate Europe Ltd.
Unit 1, Heathcote Business Centre, Hurlbutt Road
Warwick, Warwickshire CV34 6TD, UK

Cover image:
Kingmeata Etidlooie
Northern Spirits, 1988
Lithograph, 51 x 66.5 cm (20 1/16 x 26 3/16 in.)
Printer: Pitseolak Niviaqsi

Pomegranate Catalog No. AA290
ISBN 0-7649-3230-6

Designed by Patrice Morris

PRINTED IN KOREA

14 13 12 11 10 09 08 07 06 05   10 9 8 7 6 5 4 3 2 1

On southwestern Baffin Island in the Canadian Arctic Territory of Nunavut, the Inuit artists of Cape Dorset have been pulling prints since 1959. Various media are employed—aquatint and etching, copper engraving, woodcut, stencil—but the studios' mainstays are stonecut and lithograph.

In most cases, artists bring their drawings to the studios, where their work is transferred to stone and editioned by skilled printmakers. Artists may also work directly on a litho plate or stone, consulting with the printmakers through the proofing stage.

The studios are active from fall through late spring. When the editioning is finished, the staff leave the shops to return to the land and their traditional way of life. The Inuit are determined to retain important elements of their culture—their language and stories, their connection to the Arctic and its resources—while adapting to modern ways. (Dorset Fine Arts, the Toronto marketing office for the print studios, is a division of the West Baffin Eskimo Cooperative, which also owns and operates a grocery/hardware store, a snowmobile dealership, and a fuel delivery service.)

This address book presents forty reproductions of lithographs, etchings/aquatints, stonecuts, and stencils from the artists of the Cape Dorset studios. Elegant, eloquent, and filled with quiet power, they make a strong and buoyant statement of Inuit cultural traditions.

Kenojuak Ashevak
Deep Blue Sea, 2003
Lithograph and stencil, 76.4 x 113.5 cm (30$\frac{1}{16}$ x 44$\frac{11}{16}$ in.)
Printer: Niveaksie Quvianaqtuliaq

Iyola Kingwatsiak
Frightful Birds, 1993
Lithograph, 56.9 x 76.2 cm (22⅜ x 30 in.)
Printer: Pitseolak Niviaqsi

NAME Anfinsen, Roger; Carol.
ADDRESS
PHONE (H) 847 - 433 -1329.
PHONE (W) Message 847 - 433 -1424.
FAX
EMAIL
CELL/PAGER

NAME Anfinsen, Laurel & Nanci
ADDRESS
Nanci-work (?.) 859-6860
PHONE (H) 879-6697
PHONE (W)
FAX
EMAIL
CELL/PAGER

NAME (AAA - Villa Park)
ADDRESS
PHONE (H) 630 - 834 - 5923
PHONE (W)
FAX
EMAIL
CELL/PAGER

NAME
ADDRESS
PHONE (H)
PHONE (W)
FAX
EMAIL
CELL/PAGER

NAME
ADDRESS
PHONE (H)
PHONE (W)
FAX
EMAIL
CELL/PAGER

NAME
ADDRESS
PHONE (H)
PHONE (W)
FAX
EMAIL
CELL/PAGER

NAME Janet Abri (Tony)

ADDRESS 800 Spring Valley Court.
Schaumberg, Il 60193

EMAIL

PHONE (H) 847-524-5867

PHONE (W)

FAX

CELL/PAGER

NAME Ralph Antinsen

ADDRESS 6318 Hatsra Ct.

EMAIL

PHONE (H)

PHONE (W)

FAX

CELL/PAGER

NAME

ADDRESS

EMAIL

PHONE (H)

PHONE (W)

FAX

CELL/PAGER

NAME

ADDRESS

EMAIL

PHONE (H)

PHONE (W)

FAX

CELL/PAGER

NAME

ADDRESS

EMAIL

PHONE (H)

PHONE (W)

FAX

CELL/PAGER

NAME

ADDRESS

EMAIL

PHONE (H)

PHONE (W)

FAX

CELL/PAGER

NAME		PHONE (H)	
ADDRESS		PHONE (W)	
		FAX	
EMAIL		CELL/PAGER	

NAME		PHONE (H)	
ADDRESS		PHONE (W)	
		FAX	
EMAIL		CELL/PAGER	

NAME		PHONE (H)	
ADDRESS		PHONE (W)	
		FAX	
EMAIL		CELL/PAGER	

NAME		PHONE (H)	
ADDRESS		PHONE (W)	
		FAX	
EMAIL		CELL/PAGER	

NAME		PHONE (H)	
ADDRESS		PHONE (W)	
		FAX	
EMAIL		CELL/PAGER	

NAME		PHONE (H)	
ADDRESS		PHONE (W)	
		FAX	
EMAIL		CELL/PAGER	

NAME

ADDRESS

EMAIL

PHONE (H)

PHONE (W)

FAX

CELL/PAGER

NAME

ADDRESS

EMAIL

PHONE (H)

PHONE (W)

FAX

CELL/PAGER

NAME

ADDRESS

EMAIL

PHONE (H)

PHONE (W)

FAX

CELL/PAGER

NAME

ADDRESS

EMAIL

PHONE (H)

PHONE (W)

FAX

CELL/PAGER

NAME

ADDRESS

EMAIL

PHONE (H)

PHONE (W)

FAX

CELL/PAGER

NAME

ADDRESS

EMAIL

PHONE (H)

PHONE (W)

FAX

CELL/PAGER

Kavavaow Mannomee
Qupanuaq (Snow Bunting), 1993
Stonecut and stencil, 49.4 x 62.1 cm (19⁷⁄₁₆ x 24⁷⁄₁₆ in.)
Printer: Arnaqu Ashevak

Kavavaow Mannomee
Blue Bird, 1993
Lithograph and stencil, 76.3 x 56.8 cm (30 x 22⅜ in.)
Printer: Niveaksie Quvianaqtuliaq

NAME Ralph & Ann Burns
Nancy (Grady) Boles

ADDRESS 267 S. Richmond Ave.
Clarendon Hills, Il. 60514

EMAIL

PHONE (H) 789-2062
PHONE (W)
FAX
CELL/PAGER

NAME Nancy & Grady Boles.

ADDRESS 854 Saddlewood
G.E.

EMAIL

PHONE (H) 469-0572
PHONE (W)
FAX
CELL/PAGER

NAME

ADDRESS

EMAIL

PHONE (H)
PHONE (W)
FAX
CELL/PAGER

NAME

ADDRESS

EMAIL

PHONE (H)
PHONE (W)
FAX
CELL/PAGER

NAME

ADDRESS

EMAIL

PHONE (H)
PHONE (W)
FAX
CELL/PAGER

NAME

ADDRESS

EMAIL

PHONE (H)
PHONE (W)
FAX
CELL/PAGER

NAME Dick & Joyce Bridgeman	PHONE (H) (623) - 412 -
ADDRESS 7671 West Mary Jane Lane	PHONE (W) 3072
Peoria, Ariz.	FAX
EMAIL 85382	CELL/PAGER

NAME Sally Barnier	PHONE (H)
ADDRESS	PHONE (W)
WK? 245-2481	FAX
EMAIL	CELL/PAGER

NAME	PHONE (H)
ADDRESS	PHONE (W)
	FAX
EMAIL	CELL/PAGER

NAME	PHONE (H)
ADDRESS	PHONE (W)
	FAX
EMAIL	CELL/PAGER

NAME	PHONE (H)
ADDRESS	PHONE (W)
	FAX
EMAIL	CELL/PAGER

NAME	PHONE (H)
ADDRESS	PHONE (W)
	FAX
EMAIL	CELL/PAGER

NAME Tad's Becka Borwick

PHONE (H)

ADDRESS cell phone 517-331-5454

PHONE (W)

FAX

EMAIL

CELL/PAGER

NAME Beringer, Connie

PHONE (H)

ADDRESS

PHONE (W)

FAX

EMAIL 547-1447

CELL/PAGER

NAME

PHONE (H)

ADDRESS

PHONE (W)

FAX

EMAIL

CELL/PAGER

NAME

PHONE (H)

ADDRESS

PHONE (W)

FAX

EMAIL

CELL/PAGER

NAME

PHONE (H)

ADDRESS

PHONE (W)

FAX

EMAIL

CELL/PAGER

NAME

PHONE (H)

ADDRESS

PHONE (W)

FAX

EMAIL

CELL/PAGER

NAME

ADDRESS

EMAIL

PHONE (H)

PHONE (W)

FAX

CELL/PAGER

NAME

ADDRESS

EMAIL

PHONE (H)

PHONE (W)

FAX

CELL/PAGER

NAME

ADDRESS

EMAIL

PHONE (H)

PHONE (W)

FAX

CELL/PAGER

NAME

ADDRESS

EMAIL

PHONE (H)

PHONE (W)

FAX

CELL/PAGER

NAME

ADDRESS

EMAIL

PHONE (H)

PHONE (W)

FAX

CELL/PAGER

NAME

ADDRESS

EMAIL

PHONE (H)

PHONE (W)

FAX

CELL/PAGER

Kananginak Pootoogook
Calling the Pups, 1992
Lithograph and stencil, 56.5 x 71.2 cm (22¼ x 28 in.)
Printer: Pitseolak Niviaqsi

Mayoreak Ashoona
Matching Braids, 1991
Lithograph and stencil, 51.3 x 56.5 cm (20³⁄₁₆ x 21¼ in.)
Printer: Aoudla Pudlat

NAME Carol & Bob Charniak **PHONE (H)** 858-3946
ADDRESS 86 N. Main **PHONE (W)**

FAX

EMAIL Mike, Sova — Toby **CELL/PAGER**

NAME Cynthia & Joe Cevvone **PHONE (H)** 469-3019
ADDRESS 440 Elm. **PHONE (W)**

FAX

EMAIL cevuonec @ aol.com. **CELL/PAGER**

NAME Charniak - Carol work — **PHONE (H)**
ADDRESS 477 E. Butterfield Road **PHONE (W)**
Suite 101 — Lombard IL 60148 **FAX**
EMAIL (630) - 852 - 1800 **CELL/PAGER**

NAME **PHONE (H)**
ADDRESS **PHONE (W)**

FAX

EMAIL **CELL/PAGER**

NAME **PHONE (H)**
ADDRESS **PHONE (W)**

FAX

EMAIL **CELL/PAGER**

NAME **PHONE (H)**
ADDRESS **PHONE (W)**

FAX

EMAIL **CELL/PAGER**

NAME

ADDRESS

EMAIL

PHONE (H)

PHONE (W)

FAX

CELL/PAGER

NAME

ADDRESS

EMAIL

PHONE (H)

PHONE (W)

FAX

CELL/PAGER

NAME

ADDRESS

EMAIL

PHONE (H)

PHONE (W)

FAX

CELL/PAGER

NAME

ADDRESS

EMAIL

PHONE (H)

PHONE (W)

FAX

CELL/PAGER

NAME

ADDRESS

EMAIL

PHONE (H)

PHONE (W)

FAX

CELL/PAGER

NAME

ADDRESS

EMAIL

PHONE (H)

PHONE (W)

FAX

CELL/PAGER

NAME	PHONE (H)
ADDRESS	PHONE (W)
	FAX
EMAIL	CELL/PAGER

NAME	PHONE (H)
ADDRESS	PHONE (W)
	FAX
EMAIL	CELL/PAGER

NAME	PHONE (H)
ADDRESS	PHONE (W)
	FAX
EMAIL	CELL/PAGER

NAME	PHONE (H)
ADDRESS	PHONE (W)
	FAX
EMAIL	CELL/PAGER

NAME	PHONE (H)
ADDRESS	PHONE (W)
	FAX
EMAIL	CELL/PAGER

NAME	PHONE (H)
ADDRESS	PHONE (W)
	FAX
EMAIL	CELL/PAGER

NAME	PHONE (H)
ADDRESS	PHONE (W)
	FAX
EMAIL	CELL/PAGER

NAME	PHONE (H)
ADDRESS	PHONE (W)
	FAX
EMAIL	CELL/PAGER

NAME	PHONE (H)
ADDRESS	PHONE (W)
	FAX
EMAIL	CELL/PAGER

NAME	PHONE (H)
ADDRESS	PHONE (W)
	FAX
EMAIL	CELL/PAGER

NAME	PHONE (H)
ADDRESS	PHONE (W)
	FAX
EMAIL	CELL/PAGER

NAME	PHONE (H)
ADDRESS	PHONE (W)
	FAX
EMAIL	CELL/PAGER

Pudlo Pudlat
Overshadowed by a Great Bird, 1985
Lithograph, 56.5 x 75.5 cm (22¼ x 29¾ in.)
Printer: Pootoogook Keatshuk

Pitseolak Ashoona
The River at Netsiilik, 1982
Lithograph, 66.5 x 51 cm (26³⁄₁₆ x 20¹⁄₁₆ in.)
Printer: Pitseolak Niviaqsi

NAME _____ PHONE (H) _____

ADDRESS _____ PHONE (W) _____

_____ FAX _____

EMAIL _____ CELL/PAGER _____

NAME _____ PHONE (H) _____

ADDRESS _____ PHONE (W) _____

_____ FAX _____

EMAIL _____ CELL/PAGER _____

NAME _____ PHONE (H) _____

ADDRESS _____ PHONE (W) _____

_____ FAX _____

EMAIL _____ CELL/PAGER _____

NAME _____ PHONE (H) _____

ADDRESS _____ PHONE (W) _____

_____ FAX _____

EMAIL _____ CELL/PAGER _____

NAME _____ PHONE (H) _____

ADDRESS _____ PHONE (W) _____

_____ FAX _____

EMAIL _____ CELL/PAGER _____

NAME _____ PHONE (H) _____

ADDRESS _____ PHONE (W) _____

_____ FAX _____

EMAIL _____ CELL/PAGER _____

NAME

ADDRESS

EMAIL

PHONE (H)

PHONE (W)

FAX

CELL/PAGER

NAME

ADDRESS

EMAIL

PHONE (H)

PHONE (W)

FAX

CELL/PAGER

NAME

ADDRESS

EMAIL

PHONE (H)

PHONE (W)

FAX

CELL/PAGER

NAME

ADDRESS

EMAIL

PHONE (H)

PHONE (W)

FAX

CELL/PAGER

NAME

ADDRESS

EMAIL

PHONE (H)

PHONE (W)

FAX

CELL/PAGER

NAME

ADDRESS

EMAIL

PHONE (H)

PHONE (W)

FAX

CELL/PAGER

NAME

ADDRESS

EMAIL

PHONE (H)

PHONE (W)

FAX

CELL/PAGER

NAME

ADDRESS

EMAIL

PHONE (H)

PHONE (W)

FAX

CELL/PAGER

NAME

ADDRESS

EMAIL

PHONE (H)

PHONE (W)

FAX

CELL/PAGER

NAME

ADDRESS

EMAIL

PHONE (H)

PHONE (W)

FAX

CELL/PAGER

NAME

ADDRESS

EMAIL

PHONE (H)

PHONE (W)

FAX

CELL/PAGER

NAME

ADDRESS

EMAIL

PHONE (H)

PHONE (W)

FAX

CELL/PAGER

NAME

ADDRESS

EMAIL

PHONE (H)

PHONE (W)

FAX

CELL/PAGER

NAME

ADDRESS

EMAIL

PHONE (H)

PHONE (W)

FAX

CELL/PAGER

NAME

ADDRESS

EMAIL

PHONE (H)

PHONE (W)

FAX

CELL/PAGER

NAME

ADDRESS

EMAIL

PHONE (H)

PHONE (W)

FAX

CELL/PAGER

NAME

ADDRESS

EMAIL

PHONE (H)

PHONE (W)

FAX

CELL/PAGER

NAME

ADDRESS

EMAIL

PHONE (H)

PHONE (W)

FAX

CELL/PAGER

Pitseolak Ashoona
Moonlight, 1982
Lithograph, 51.5 x 66 cm (20¼ x 26 in.)
Printer: Pitseolak Niviaqsi

Eegyvudluk Ragee
Angako Quviasuktu (Happy Shaman), 1981
Stonecut and stencil, 56 x 76.5 cm (22 1/16 x 30 1/8 in.)
Printer: Saggiaktok Saggiaktok

NAME	PHONE (H)
ADDRESS	PHONE (W)
	FAX
EMAIL	CELL/PAGER

NAME	PHONE (H)
ADDRESS	PHONE (W)
	FAX
EMAIL	CELL/PAGER

NAME	PHONE (H)
ADDRESS	PHONE (W)
	FAX
EMAIL	CELL/PAGER

NAME	PHONE (H)
ADDRESS	PHONE (W)
	FAX
EMAIL	CELL/PAGER

NAME	PHONE (H)
ADDRESS	PHONE (W)
	FAX
EMAIL	CELL/PAGER

NAME	PHONE (H)
ADDRESS	PHONE (W)
	FAX
EMAIL	CELL/PAGER

NAME

ADDRESS

EMAIL

PHONE (H)

PHONE (W)

FAX

CELL/PAGER

NAME

ADDRESS

EMAIL

PHONE (H)

PHONE (W)

FAX

CELL/PAGER

NAME

ADDRESS

EMAIL

PHONE (H)

PHONE (W)

FAX

CELL/PAGER

NAME

ADDRESS

EMAIL

PHONE (H)

PHONE (W)

FAX

CELL/PAGER

NAME

ADDRESS

EMAIL

PHONE (H)

PHONE (W)

FAX

CELL/PAGER

NAME

ADDRESS

EMAIL

PHONE (H)

PHONE (W)

FAX

CELL/PAGER

NAME

ADDRESS

EMAIL

PHONE (H)

PHONE (W)

FAX

CELL/PAGER

NAME

ADDRESS

EMAIL

PHONE (H)

PHONE (W)

FAX

CELL/PAGER

NAME

ADDRESS

EMAIL

PHONE (H)

PHONE (W)

FAX

CELL/PAGER

NAME

ADDRESS

EMAIL

PHONE (H)

PHONE (W)

FAX

CELL/PAGER

NAME

ADDRESS

EMAIL

PHONE (H)

PHONE (W)

FAX

CELL/PAGER

NAME

ADDRESS

EMAIL

PHONE (H)

PHONE (W)

FAX

CELL/PAGER

NAME	PHONE (H)
ADDRESS	PHONE (W)
	FAX
EMAIL	CELL/PAGER

NAME	PHONE (H)
ADDRESS	PHONE (W)
	FAX
EMAIL	CELL/PAGER

NAME	PHONE (H)
ADDRESS	PHONE (W)
	FAX
EMAIL	CELL/PAGER

NAME	PHONE (H)
ADDRESS	PHONE (W)
	FAX
EMAIL	CELL/PAGER

NAME	PHONE (H)
ADDRESS	PHONE (W)
	FAX
EMAIL	CELL/PAGER

NAME	PHONE (H)
ADDRESS	PHONE (W)
	FAX
EMAIL	CELL/PAGER

Mary Pudlat
Riding on a Kanayuk, 1980
Stonecut and stencil, 46 x 60.5 cm (18⅛ x 23¹³⁄₁₆ in.)
Printer: Ningeoseak Pudlat

Mayoreak Ashoona
Walrus with Young, 1980
Lithograph, 49.5 x 56.5 cm (19½ x 22¼ in.)
Printer: Aoudla Pudlat

NAME

ADDRESS

EMAIL

PHONE (H)

PHONE (W)

FAX

CELL/PAGER

NAME

ADDRESS

EMAIL

PHONE (H)

PHONE (W)

FAX

CELL/PAGER

NAME

ADDRESS

EMAIL

PHONE (H)

PHONE (W)

FAX

CELL/PAGER

NAME

ADDRESS

EMAIL

PHONE (H)

PHONE (W)

FAX

CELL/PAGER

NAME

ADDRESS

EMAIL

PHONE (H)

PHONE (W)

FAX

CELL/PAGER

NAME

ADDRESS

EMAIL

PHONE (H)

PHONE (W)

FAX

CELL/PAGER

NAME

PHONE (H)

ADDRESS

PHONE (W)

FAX

EMAIL

CELL/PAGER

NAME

PHONE (H)

ADDRESS

PHONE (W)

FAX

EMAIL

CELL/PAGER

NAME

PHONE (H)

ADDRESS

PHONE (W)

FAX

EMAIL

CELL/PAGER

NAME

PHONE (H)

ADDRESS

PHONE (W)

FAX

EMAIL

CELL/PAGER

NAME

PHONE (H)

ADDRESS

PHONE (W)

FAX

EMAIL

CELL/PAGER

NAME

PHONE (H)

ADDRESS

PHONE (W)

FAX

EMAIL

CELL/PAGER

NAME

ADDRESS

EMAIL

PHONE (H)

PHONE (W)

FAX

CELL/PAGER

NAME

ADDRESS

EMAIL

PHONE (H)

PHONE (W)

FAX

CELL/PAGER

NAME

ADDRESS

EMAIL

PHONE (H)

PHONE (W)

FAX

CELL/PAGER

NAME

ADDRESS

EMAIL

PHONE (H)

PHONE (W)

FAX

CELL/PAGER

NAME

ADDRESS

EMAIL

PHONE (H)

PHONE (W)

FAX

CELL/PAGER

NAME

ADDRESS

EMAIL

PHONE (H)

PHONE (W)

FAX

CELL/PAGER

NAME	PHONE (H)
ADDRESS	PHONE (W)
	FAX
EMAIL	CELL/PAGER

NAME	PHONE (H)
ADDRESS	PHONE (W)
	FAX
EMAIL	CELL/PAGER

NAME	PHONE (H)
ADDRESS	PHONE (W)
	FAX
EMAIL	CELL/PAGER

NAME	PHONE (H)
ADDRESS	PHONE (W)
	FAX
EMAIL	CELL/PAGER

NAME	PHONE (H)
ADDRESS	PHONE (W)
	FAX
EMAIL	CELL/PAGER

NAME	PHONE (H)
ADDRESS	PHONE (W)
	FAX
EMAIL	CELL/PAGER

Kenojuak Ashevak
The Harbinger, 1993
Stonecut and stencil, 49.4 x 62.4 cm (19½ x 24½ in.)
Printer: Pee Mikiga

Kavavaow Mannomee
Young Goose Preening, 1990
Stonecut and stencil, 64 x 46.8 cm (25 x 18½ in.)
Printer: Kavavaow Mannomee

NAME

ADDRESS

EMAIL

PHONE (H)

PHONE (W)

FAX

CELL/PAGER

NAME

ADDRESS

EMAIL

PHONE (H)

PHONE (W)

FAX

CELL/PAGER

NAME

ADDRESS

EMAIL

PHONE (H)

PHONE (W)

FAX

CELL/PAGER

NAME

ADDRESS

EMAIL

PHONE (H)

PHONE (W)

FAX

CELL/PAGER

NAME

ADDRESS

EMAIL

PHONE (H)

PHONE (W)

FAX

CELL/PAGER

NAME

ADDRESS

EMAIL

PHONE (H)

PHONE (W)

FAX

CELL/PAGER

NAME _____ PHONE (H) _____

ADDRESS _____ PHONE (W) _____

_____ FAX _____

EMAIL _____ CELL/PAGER _____

NAME _____ PHONE (H) _____

ADDRESS _____ PHONE (W) _____

_____ FAX _____

EMAIL _____ CELL/PAGER _____

NAME _____ PHONE (H) _____

ADDRESS _____ PHONE (W) _____

_____ FAX _____

EMAIL _____ CELL/PAGER _____

NAME _____ PHONE (H) _____

ADDRESS _____ PHONE (W) _____

_____ FAX _____

EMAIL _____ CELL/PAGER _____

NAME _____ PHONE (H) _____

ADDRESS _____ PHONE (W) _____

_____ FAX _____

EMAIL _____ CELL/PAGER _____

NAME _____ PHONE (H) _____

ADDRESS _____ PHONE (W) _____

_____ FAX _____

EMAIL _____ CELL/PAGER _____

NAME	PHONE (H)
ADDRESS	PHONE (W)
	FAX
EMAIL	CELL/PAGER

NAME	PHONE (H)
ADDRESS	PHONE (W)
	FAX
EMAIL	CELL/PAGER

NAME	PHONE (H)
ADDRESS	PHONE (W)
	FAX
EMAIL	CELL/PAGER

NAME	PHONE (H)
ADDRESS	PHONE (W)
	FAX
EMAIL	CELL/PAGER

NAME	PHONE (H)
ADDRESS	PHONE (W)
	FAX
EMAIL	CELL/PAGER

NAME	PHONE (H)
ADDRESS	PHONE (W)
	FAX
EMAIL	CELL/PAGER

NAME	PHONE (H)
ADDRESS	PHONE (W)
	FAX
EMAIL	CELL/PAGER

NAME	PHONE (H)
ADDRESS	PHONE (W)
	FAX
EMAIL	CELL/PAGER

NAME	PHONE (H)
ADDRESS	PHONE (W)
	FAX
EMAIL	CELL/PAGER

NAME	PHONE (H)
ADDRESS	PHONE (W)
	FAX
EMAIL	CELL/PAGER

NAME	PHONE (H)
ADDRESS	PHONE (W)
	FAX
EMAIL	CELL/PAGER

NAME	PHONE (H)
ADDRESS	PHONE (W)
	FAX
EMAIL	CELL/PAGER

Meelia Kelly
Illauliutit (Caribou Herd), 2001
Stonecut, 62 x 49.8 cm (24⅜ x 19⅝ in.)
Printer: Qiatsuq Niviaqsi

Kananginak Pootoogook
Approaching Storm, 2002
Lithograph, 71.7 x 57 cm (28¼ x 22⁷⁄₁₆ in.)
Printer: Niviaksie Quvianaqtuliaq

NAME

ADDRESS

EMAIL

PHONE (H)

PHONE (W)

FAX

CELL/PAGER

NAME

ADDRESS

EMAIL

PHONE (H)

PHONE (W)

FAX

CELL/PAGER

NAME

ADDRESS

EMAIL

PHONE (H)

PHONE (W)

FAX

CELL/PAGER

NAME

ADDRESS

EMAIL

PHONE (H)

PHONE (W)

FAX

CELL/PAGER

NAME

ADDRESS

EMAIL

PHONE (H)

PHONE (W)

FAX

CELL/PAGER

NAME

ADDRESS

EMAIL

PHONE (H)

PHONE (W)

FAX

CELL/PAGER

NAME

PHONE (H)

ADDRESS

PHONE (W)

FAX

EMAIL

CELL/PAGER

NAME

PHONE (H)

ADDRESS

PHONE (W)

FAX

EMAIL

CELL/PAGER

NAME

PHONE (H)

ADDRESS

PHONE (W)

FAX

EMAIL

CELL/PAGER

NAME

PHONE (H)

ADDRESS

PHONE (W)

FAX

EMAIL

CELL/PAGER

NAME

PHONE (H)

ADDRESS

PHONE (W)

FAX

EMAIL

CELL/PAGER

NAME

PHONE (H)

ADDRESS

PHONE (W)

FAX

EMAIL

CELL/PAGER

NAME	PHONE (H)
ADDRESS	PHONE (W)
	FAX
EMAIL	CELL/PAGER

NAME	PHONE (H)
ADDRESS	PHONE (W)
	FAX
EMAIL	CELL/PAGER

NAME	PHONE (H)
ADDRESS	PHONE (W)
	FAX
EMAIL	CELL/PAGER

NAME	PHONE (H)
ADDRESS	PHONE (W)
	FAX
EMAIL	CELL/PAGER

NAME	PHONE (H)
ADDRESS	PHONE (W)
	FAX
EMAIL	CELL/PAGER

NAME	PHONE (H)
ADDRESS	PHONE (W)
	FAX
EMAIL	CELL/PAGER

NAME	PHONE (H)
ADDRESS	PHONE (W)
	FAX
EMAIL	CELL/PAGER

NAME	PHONE (H)
ADDRESS	PHONE (W)
	FAX
EMAIL	CELL/PAGER

NAME	PHONE (H)
ADDRESS	PHONE (W)
	FAX
EMAIL	CELL/PAGER

NAME	PHONE (H)
ADDRESS	PHONE (W)
	FAX
EMAIL	CELL/PAGER

NAME	PHONE (H)
ADDRESS	PHONE (W)
	FAX
EMAIL	CELL/PAGER

NAME	PHONE (H)
ADDRESS	PHONE (W)
	FAX
EMAIL	CELL/PAGER

Pitaloosie Saila
Ipiraqtuqtuq, 1976
Lithograph, 76.2 x 55.9 cm (30 x 22 in.)
Printer: Pitseolak Niviaqsi

Anirnik Oshuitoq
Ravens of the Spirit World, 1982
Lithograph, 51.6 x 66.1 cm (20⁵⁄₁₆ x 26 in.)
Printer: Pitseolak Niviaqsi

NAME

ADDRESS

EMAIL

PHONE (H)

PHONE (W)

FAX

CELL/PAGER

NAME

ADDRESS

EMAIL

PHONE (H)

PHONE (W)

FAX

CELL/PAGER

NAME

ADDRESS

EMAIL

PHONE (H)

PHONE (W)

FAX

CELL/PAGER

NAME

ADDRESS

EMAIL

PHONE (H)

PHONE (W)

FAX

CELL/PAGER

NAME

ADDRESS

EMAIL

PHONE (H)

PHONE (W)

FAX

CELL/PAGER

NAME

ADDRESS

EMAIL

PHONE (H)

PHONE (W)

FAX

CELL/PAGER

NAME _____ PHONE (H) _____

ADDRESS _____ PHONE (W) _____

_____ FAX _____

EMAIL _____ CELL/PAGER _____

NAME _____ PHONE (H) _____

ADDRESS _____ PHONE (W) _____

_____ FAX _____

EMAIL _____ CELL/PAGER _____

NAME _____ PHONE (H) _____

ADDRESS _____ PHONE (W) _____

_____ FAX _____

EMAIL _____ CELL/PAGER _____

NAME _____ PHONE (H) _____

ADDRESS _____ PHONE (W) _____

_____ FAX _____

EMAIL _____ CELL/PAGER _____

NAME _____ PHONE (H) _____

ADDRESS _____ PHONE (W) _____

_____ FAX _____

EMAIL _____ CELL/PAGER _____

NAME _____ PHONE (H) _____

ADDRESS _____ PHONE (W) _____

_____ FAX _____

EMAIL _____ CELL/PAGER _____

NAME

ADDRESS

EMAIL

PHONE (H)

PHONE (W)

FAX

CELL/PAGER

NAME

ADDRESS

EMAIL

PHONE (H)

PHONE (W)

FAX

CELL/PAGER

NAME

ADDRESS

EMAIL

PHONE (H)

PHONE (W)

FAX

CELL/PAGER

NAME

ADDRESS

EMAIL

PHONE (H)

PHONE (W)

FAX

CELL/PAGER

NAME

ADDRESS

EMAIL

PHONE (H)

PHONE (W)

FAX

CELL/PAGER

NAME

ADDRESS

EMAIL

PHONE (H)

PHONE (W)

FAX

CELL/PAGER

NAME _____

PHONE (H) _____

ADDRESS _____

PHONE (W) _____

_____

FAX _____

EMAIL _____

CELL/PAGER _____

NAME _____

PHONE (H) _____

ADDRESS _____

PHONE (W) _____

_____

FAX _____

EMAIL _____

CELL/PAGER _____

NAME _____

PHONE (H) _____

ADDRESS _____

PHONE (W) _____

_____

FAX _____

EMAIL _____

CELL/PAGER _____

NAME _____

PHONE (H) _____

ADDRESS _____

PHONE (W) _____

_____

FAX _____

EMAIL _____

CELL/PAGER _____

NAME _____

PHONE (H) _____

ADDRESS _____

PHONE (W) _____

_____

FAX _____

EMAIL _____

CELL/PAGER _____

NAME _____

PHONE (H) _____

ADDRESS _____

PHONE (W) _____

_____

FAX _____

EMAIL _____

CELL/PAGER _____

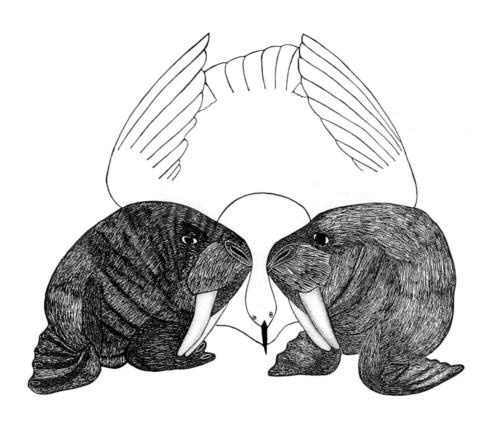

Mayoreak Ashoona
Walrus and Bird, 1994
Stonecut and stencil, 62.1 x 76.3 cm (24⁷⁄₁₆ x 30¹⁄₁₆ in.)
Printer: Pee Mikiga

Ohotaq Mikkigak
Curious Owl, 2003
Stonecut and stencil, 62 x 76.2 cm (24⅜ x 30 in.)
Printer: Arnaqu Ashevak

NAME

ADDRESS

EMAIL

PHONE (H)

PHONE (W)

FAX

CELL/PAGER

NAME

ADDRESS

EMAIL

PHONE (H)

PHONE (W)

FAX

CELL/PAGER

NAME

ADDRESS

EMAIL

PHONE (H)

PHONE (W)

FAX

CELL/PAGER

NAME

ADDRESS

EMAIL

PHONE (H)

PHONE (W)

FAX

CELL/PAGER

NAME

ADDRESS

EMAIL

PHONE (H)

PHONE (W)

FAX

CELL/PAGER

NAME

ADDRESS

EMAIL

PHONE (H)

PHONE (W)

FAX

CELL/PAGER

NAME

PHONE (H)

ADDRESS

PHONE (W)

FAX

EMAIL

CELL/PAGER

NAME

PHONE (H)

ADDRESS

PHONE (W)

FAX

EMAIL

CELL/PAGER

NAME

PHONE (H)

ADDRESS

PHONE (W)

FAX

EMAIL

CELL/PAGER

NAME

PHONE (H)

ADDRESS

PHONE (W)

FAX

EMAIL

CELL/PAGER

NAME

PHONE (H)

ADDRESS

PHONE (W)

FAX

EMAIL

CELL/PAGER

NAME

PHONE (H)

ADDRESS

PHONE (W)

FAX

EMAIL

CELL/PAGER

NAME	PHONE (H)
ADDRESS	PHONE (W)
	FAX
EMAIL	CELL/PAGER

NAME	PHONE (H)
ADDRESS	PHONE (W)
	FAX
EMAIL	CELL/PAGER

NAME	PHONE (H)
ADDRESS	PHONE (W)
	FAX
EMAIL	CELL/PAGER

NAME	PHONE (H)
ADDRESS	PHONE (W)
	FAX
EMAIL	CELL/PAGER

NAME	PHONE (H)
ADDRESS	PHONE (W)
	FAX
EMAIL	CELL/PAGER

NAME	PHONE (H)
ADDRESS	PHONE (W)
	FAX
EMAIL	CELL/PAGER

NAME	PHONE (H)
ADDRESS	PHONE (W)
	FAX
EMAIL	CELL/PAGER

NAME	PHONE (H)
ADDRESS	PHONE (W)
	FAX
EMAIL	CELL/PAGER

NAME	PHONE (H)
ADDRESS	PHONE (W)
	FAX
EMAIL	CELL/PAGER

NAME	PHONE (H)
ADDRESS	PHONE (W)
	FAX
EMAIL	CELL/PAGER

NAME	PHONE (H)
ADDRESS	PHONE (W)
	FAX
EMAIL	CELL/PAGER

NAME	PHONE (H)
ADDRESS	PHONE (W)
	FAX
EMAIL	CELL/PAGER

Mary Pudlat
Woman Gathering Kelp, 1997
Lithograph, 77 x 57 cm (30 5/16 x 22 7/16 in.)
Printer: Pitseolak Niviaqsi

Ohotaq Mikkigak
Ascending Loon, 2003
Stonecut and stencil, 64 x 79 cm (25³⁄₁₆ x 31⅛ in.)
Printer: Kavavaow Mannomee

NAME

PHONE (H)

ADDRESS

PHONE (W)

FAX

EMAIL

CELL/PAGER

NAME

PHONE (H)

ADDRESS

PHONE (W)

FAX

EMAIL

CELL/PAGER

NAME

PHONE (H)

ADDRESS

PHONE (W)

FAX

EMAIL

CELL/PAGER

NAME

PHONE (H)

ADDRESS

PHONE (W)

FAX

EMAIL

CELL/PAGER

NAME

PHONE (H)

ADDRESS

PHONE (W)

FAX

EMAIL

CELL/PAGER

NAME

PHONE (H)

ADDRESS

PHONE (W)

FAX

EMAIL

CELL/PAGER

NAME _____   PHONE (H) _____

ADDRESS _____   PHONE (W) _____

_____   FAX _____

EMAIL _____   CELL/PAGER _____

NAME _____   PHONE (H) _____

ADDRESS _____   PHONE (W) _____

_____   FAX _____

EMAIL _____   CELL/PAGER _____

NAME _____   PHONE (H) _____

ADDRESS _____   PHONE (W) _____

_____   FAX _____

EMAIL _____   CELL/PAGER _____

NAME _____   PHONE (H) _____

ADDRESS _____   PHONE (W) _____

_____   FAX _____

EMAIL _____   CELL/PAGER _____

NAME _____   PHONE (H) _____

ADDRESS _____   PHONE (W) _____

_____   FAX _____

EMAIL _____   CELL/PAGER _____

NAME _____   PHONE (H) _____

ADDRESS _____   PHONE (W) _____

_____   FAX _____

EMAIL _____   CELL/PAGER _____

NAME _____ PHONE (H) _____

ADDRESS _____ PHONE (W) _____

_____ FAX _____

EMAIL _____ CELL/PAGER _____

NAME _____ PHONE (H) _____

ADDRESS _____ PHONE (W) _____

_____ FAX _____

EMAIL _____ CELL/PAGER _____

NAME _____ PHONE (H) _____

ADDRESS _____ PHONE (W) _____

_____ FAX _____

EMAIL _____ CELL/PAGER _____

NAME _____ PHONE (H) _____

ADDRESS _____ PHONE (W) _____

_____ FAX _____

EMAIL _____ CELL/PAGER _____

NAME _____ PHONE (H) _____

ADDRESS _____ PHONE (W) _____

_____ FAX _____

EMAIL _____ CELL/PAGER _____

NAME _____ PHONE (H) _____

ADDRESS _____ PHONE (W) _____

_____ FAX _____

EMAIL _____ CELL/PAGER _____

NAME

PHONE (H)

ADDRESS

PHONE (W)

FAX

EMAIL

CELL/PAGER

NAME

PHONE (H)

ADDRESS

PHONE (W)

FAX

EMAIL

CELL/PAGER

NAME

PHONE (H)

ADDRESS

PHONE (W)

FAX

EMAIL

CELL/PAGER

NAME

PHONE (H)

ADDRESS

PHONE (W)

FAX

EMAIL

CELL/PAGER

NAME

PHONE (H)

ADDRESS

PHONE (W)

FAX

EMAIL

CELL/PAGER

NAME

PHONE (H)

ADDRESS

PHONE (W)

FAX

EMAIL

CELL/PAGER

Kananginak Pootoogook
Angujjuaq (Great Big Bear), 2003
Lithograph and stencil, 102 x 71.2 cm (40⅛ x 28 in.)
Printer: Pitseolak Niviaqsi

N

Kingmeata Etidlooie
Northern Spirits, 1988
Lithograph, 51 x 66.5 cm (20¹/₁₆ x 26³/₁₆ in.)
Printer: Pitseolak Niviaqsi

NAME

PHONE (H)

ADDRESS

PHONE (W)

FAX

EMAIL

CELL/PAGER

NAME

PHONE (H)

ADDRESS

PHONE (W)

FAX

EMAIL

CELL/PAGER

NAME

PHONE (H)

ADDRESS

PHONE (W)

FAX

EMAIL

CELL/PAGER

NAME

PHONE (H)

ADDRESS

PHONE (W)

FAX

EMAIL

CELL/PAGER

NAME

PHONE (H)

ADDRESS

PHONE (W)

FAX

EMAIL

CELL/PAGER

NAME

PHONE (H)

ADDRESS

PHONE (W)

FAX

EMAIL

CELL/PAGER

NAME

ADDRESS

EMAIL

PHONE (H)

PHONE (W)

FAX

CELL/PAGER

NAME

ADDRESS

EMAIL

PHONE (H)

PHONE (W)

FAX

CELL/PAGER

NAME

ADDRESS

EMAIL

PHONE (H)

PHONE (W)

FAX

CELL/PAGER

NAME

ADDRESS

EMAIL

PHONE (H)

PHONE (W)

FAX

CELL/PAGER

NAME

ADDRESS

EMAIL

PHONE (H)

PHONE (W)

FAX

CELL/PAGER

NAME

ADDRESS

EMAIL

PHONE (H)

PHONE (W)

FAX

CELL/PAGER

NAME

ADDRESS

PHONE (H)

PHONE (W)

FAX

EMAIL

CELL/PAGER

NAME

ADDRESS

PHONE (H)

PHONE (W)

FAX

EMAIL

CELL/PAGER

NAME

ADDRESS

PHONE (H)

PHONE (W)

FAX

EMAIL

CELL/PAGER

NAME

ADDRESS

PHONE (H)

PHONE (W)

FAX

EMAIL

CELL/PAGER

NAME

ADDRESS

PHONE (H)

PHONE (W)

FAX

EMAIL

CELL/PAGER

NAME

ADDRESS

PHONE (H)

PHONE (W)

FAX

EMAIL

CELL/PAGER

NAME

PHONE (H)

ADDRESS

PHONE (W)

FAX

EMAIL

CELL/PAGER

NAME

PHONE (H)

ADDRESS

PHONE (W)

FAX

EMAIL

CELL/PAGER

NAME

PHONE (H)

ADDRESS

PHONE (W)

FAX

EMAIL

CELL/PAGER

NAME

PHONE (H)

ADDRESS

PHONE (W)

FAX

EMAIL

CELL/PAGER

NAME

PHONE (H)

ADDRESS

PHONE (W)

FAX

EMAIL

CELL/PAGER

NAME

PHONE (H)

ADDRESS

PHONE (W)

FAX

EMAIL

CELL/PAGER

Kenojuak Ashevak
Feathered Rainbow, 2002
Lithograph, 57.4 x 76.3 cm (22⅝ x 30 in.)
Printer: Pitseolak Niviaqsi

Meelia Kelly
Battle of Wills, 2002
Stonecut, 62 x 56 cm (24⅜ x 22 1/16 in.)
Printer: Qiatsuq Niviaqsi

NAME	PHONE (H)
ADDRESS	PHONE (W)
	FAX
EMAIL	CELL/PAGER

NAME	PHONE (H)
ADDRESS	PHONE (W)
	FAX
EMAIL	CELL/PAGER

NAME	PHONE (H)
ADDRESS	PHONE (W)
	FAX
EMAIL	CELL/PAGER

NAME	PHONE (H)
ADDRESS	PHONE (W)
	FAX
EMAIL	CELL/PAGER

NAME	PHONE (H)
ADDRESS	PHONE (W)
	FAX
EMAIL	CELL/PAGER

NAME	PHONE (H)
ADDRESS	PHONE (W)
	FAX
EMAIL	CELL/PAGER

NAME

ADDRESS

EMAIL

PHONE (H)

PHONE (W)

FAX

CELL/PAGER

NAME

ADDRESS

EMAIL

PHONE (H)

PHONE (W)

FAX

CELL/PAGER

NAME

ADDRESS

EMAIL

PHONE (H)

PHONE (W)

FAX

CELL/PAGER

NAME

ADDRESS

EMAIL

PHONE (H)

PHONE (W)

FAX

CELL/PAGER

NAME

ADDRESS

EMAIL

PHONE (H)

PHONE (W)

FAX

CELL/PAGER

NAME

ADDRESS

EMAIL

PHONE (H)

PHONE (W)

FAX

CELL/PAGER

NAME

ADDRESS

EMAIL

PHONE (H)

PHONE (W)

FAX

CELL/PAGER

NAME

ADDRESS

EMAIL

PHONE (H)

PHONE (W)

FAX

CELL/PAGER

NAME

ADDRESS

EMAIL

PHONE (H)

PHONE (W)

FAX

CELL/PAGER

NAME

ADDRESS

EMAIL

PHONE (H)

PHONE (W)

FAX

CELL/PAGER

NAME

ADDRESS

EMAIL

PHONE (H)

PHONE (W)

FAX

CELL/PAGER

NAME

ADDRESS

EMAIL

PHONE (H)

PHONE (W)

FAX

CELL/PAGER

NAME

ADDRESS

EMAIL

PHONE (H)

PHONE (W)

FAX

CELL/PAGER

NAME

ADDRESS

EMAIL

PHONE (H)

PHONE (W)

FAX

CELL/PAGER

NAME

ADDRESS

EMAIL

PHONE (H)

PHONE (W)

FAX

CELL/PAGER

NAME

ADDRESS

EMAIL

PHONE (H)

PHONE (W)

FAX

CELL/PAGER

NAME

ADDRESS

EMAIL

PHONE (H)

PHONE (W)

FAX

CELL/PAGER

NAME

ADDRESS

EMAIL

PHONE (H)

PHONE (W)

FAX

CELL/PAGER

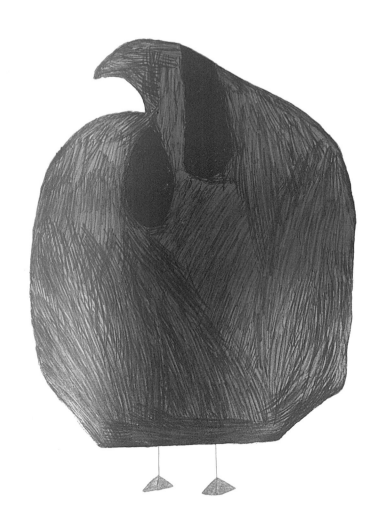

Sheojuk Etidlooie
Mitiq (Eider Duck), 1997
Lithograph, 76 x 57 cm (30 x 22½ in.)
Printer: Pitseolak Niviaqsi

P

P

Kenojuak Ashevak
Silver Owl, 1999
Etching and aquatint, 49 x 47 cm (19½ x 18½ in.)
Printer: Studio PM

NAME

PHONE (H)

ADDRESS

PHONE (W)

FAX

EMAIL

CELL/PAGER

NAME

PHONE (H)

ADDRESS

PHONE (W)

FAX

EMAIL

CELL/PAGER

NAME

PHONE (H)

ADDRESS

PHONE (W)

FAX

EMAIL

CELL/PAGER

NAME

PHONE (H)

ADDRESS

PHONE (W)

FAX

EMAIL

CELL/PAGER

NAME

PHONE (H)

ADDRESS

PHONE (W)

FAX

EMAIL

CELL/PAGER

NAME

PHONE (H)

ADDRESS

PHONE (W)

FAX

EMAIL

CELL/PAGER

NAME

ADDRESS

EMAIL

PHONE (H)

PHONE (W)

FAX

CELL/PAGER

NAME

ADDRESS

EMAIL

PHONE (H)

PHONE (W)

FAX

CELL/PAGER

NAME

ADDRESS

EMAIL

PHONE (H)

PHONE (W)

FAX

CELL/PAGER

NAME

ADDRESS

EMAIL

PHONE (H)

PHONE (W)

FAX

CELL/PAGER

NAME

ADDRESS

EMAIL

PHONE (H)

PHONE (W)

FAX

CELL/PAGER

NAME

ADDRESS

EMAIL

PHONE (H)

PHONE (W)

FAX

CELL/PAGER

NAME

ADDRESS

EMAIL

PHONE (H)

PHONE (W)

FAX

CELL/PAGER

NAME

ADDRESS

EMAIL

PHONE (H)

PHONE (W)

FAX

CELL/PAGER

NAME

ADDRESS

EMAIL

PHONE (H)

PHONE (W)

FAX

CELL/PAGER

NAME

ADDRESS

EMAIL

PHONE (H)

PHONE (W)

FAX

CELL/PAGER

NAME

ADDRESS

EMAIL

PHONE (H)

PHONE (W)

FAX

CELL/PAGER

NAME

ADDRESS

EMAIL

PHONE (H)

PHONE (W)

FAX

CELL/PAGER

NAME

ADDRESS

EMAIL

PHONE (H)

PHONE (W)

FAX

CELL/PAGER

NAME

ADDRESS

EMAIL

PHONE (H)

PHONE (W)

FAX

CELL/PAGER

NAME

ADDRESS

EMAIL

PHONE (H)

PHONE (W)

FAX

CELL/PAGER

NAME

ADDRESS

EMAIL

PHONE (H)

PHONE (W)

FAX

CELL/PAGER

NAME

ADDRESS

EMAIL

PHONE (H)

PHONE (W)

FAX

CELL/PAGER

NAME

ADDRESS

EMAIL

PHONE (H)

PHONE (W)

FAX

CELL/PAGER

Nikotai Mills
Bird Song, 1996
Lithograph, 56 x 76 cm (22 x 30 in.)
Printer: Niveaksie Quvianaqtuliaq

Kananginak Pootoogook
Panniq (Bull Caribou), 1993
Stonecut and stencil, 98.7 x 62 cm (38⅞ x 24⅜ in.)
Printer: Qiatsuq Niviaqsi

QR

NAME

ADDRESS

EMAIL

PHONE (H)

PHONE (W)

FAX

CELL/PAGER

NAME

ADDRESS

EMAIL

PHONE (H)

PHONE (W)

FAX

CELL/PAGER

NAME

ADDRESS

EMAIL

PHONE (H)

PHONE (W)

FAX

CELL/PAGER

NAME

ADDRESS

EMAIL

PHONE (H)

PHONE (W)

FAX

CELL/PAGER

NAME

ADDRESS

EMAIL

PHONE (H)

PHONE (W)

FAX

CELL/PAGER

NAME

ADDRESS

EMAIL

PHONE (H)

PHONE (W)

FAX

CELL/PAGER

NAME

ADDRESS

EMAIL

PHONE (H)

PHONE (W)

FAX

CELL/PAGER

NAME

ADDRESS

EMAIL

PHONE (H)

PHONE (W)

FAX

CELL/PAGER

NAME

ADDRESS

EMAIL

PHONE (H)

PHONE (W)

FAX

CELL/PAGER

NAME

ADDRESS

EMAIL

PHONE (H)

PHONE (W)

FAX

CELL/PAGER

NAME

ADDRESS

EMAIL

PHONE (H)

PHONE (W)

FAX

CELL/PAGER

NAME

ADDRESS

EMAIL

PHONE (H)

PHONE (W)

FAX

CELL/PAGER

NAME	PHONE (H)
ADDRESS	PHONE (W)
	FAX
EMAIL	CELL/PAGER

NAME	PHONE (H)
ADDRESS	PHONE (W)
	FAX
EMAIL	CELL/PAGER

NAME	PHONE (H)
ADDRESS	PHONE (W)
	FAX
EMAIL	CELL/PAGER

NAME	PHONE (H)
ADDRESS	PHONE (W)
	FAX
EMAIL	CELL/PAGER

NAME	PHONE (H)
ADDRESS	PHONE (W)
	FAX
EMAIL	CELL/PAGER

NAME	PHONE (H)
ADDRESS	PHONE (W)
	FAX
EMAIL	CELL/PAGER

NAME

ADDRESS

EMAIL

PHONE (H)

PHONE (W)

FAX

CELL/PAGER

NAME

ADDRESS

EMAIL

PHONE (H)

PHONE (W)

FAX

CELL/PAGER

NAME

ADDRESS

EMAIL

PHONE (H)

PHONE (W)

FAX

CELL/PAGER

NAME

ADDRESS

EMAIL

PHONE (H)

PHONE (W)

FAX

CELL/PAGER

NAME

ADDRESS

EMAIL

PHONE (H)

PHONE (W)

FAX

CELL/PAGER

NAME

ADDRESS

EMAIL

PHONE (H)

PHONE (W)

FAX

CELL/PAGER

Kananginak Pootoogook
Attiqtaliq (Bear with Cubs), 1997
Stonecut and stencil, 53 x 62 cm (20⅞ x 24⅜ in.)
Printer: Qiatsuq Niviaqsi

Nikotai Mills
Family of Owls, 1996
Etching and aquatint, 80 x 71 cm (31½ x 28 in.)
Printer: Studio PM

NAME

ADDRESS

EMAIL

PHONE (H)

PHONE (W)

FAX

CELL/PAGER

NAME

ADDRESS

EMAIL

PHONE (H)

PHONE (W)

FAX

CELL/PAGER

NAME

ADDRESS

EMAIL

PHONE (H)

PHONE (W)

FAX

CELL/PAGER

NAME

ADDRESS

EMAIL

PHONE (H)

PHONE (W)

FAX

CELL/PAGER

NAME

ADDRESS

EMAIL

PHONE (H)

PHONE (W)

FAX

CELL/PAGER

NAME

ADDRESS

EMAIL

PHONE (H)

PHONE (W)

FAX

CELL/PAGER

NAME	PHONE (H)
ADDRESS	PHONE (W)
	FAX
EMAIL	CELL/PAGER

NAME	PHONE (H)
ADDRESS	PHONE (W)
	FAX
EMAIL	CELL/PAGER

NAME	PHONE (H)
ADDRESS	PHONE (W)
	FAX
EMAIL	CELL/PAGER

NAME	PHONE (H)
ADDRESS	PHONE (W)
	FAX
EMAIL	CELL/PAGER

NAME	PHONE (H)
ADDRESS	PHONE (W)
	FAX
EMAIL	CELL/PAGER

NAME	PHONE (H)
ADDRESS	PHONE (W)
	FAX
EMAIL	CELL/PAGER

NAME	PHONE (H)
ADDRESS	PHONE (W)
	FAX
EMAIL	CELL/PAGER

NAME	PHONE (H)
ADDRESS	PHONE (W)
	FAX
EMAIL	CELL/PAGER

NAME	PHONE (H)
ADDRESS	PHONE (W)
	FAX
EMAIL	CELL/PAGER

NAME	PHONE (H)
ADDRESS	PHONE (W)
	FAX
EMAIL	CELL/PAGER

NAME	PHONE (H)
ADDRESS	PHONE (W)
	FAX
EMAIL	CELL/PAGER

NAME	PHONE (H)
ADDRESS	PHONE (W)
	FAX
EMAIL	CELL/PAGER

NAME

ADDRESS

EMAIL

PHONE (H)

PHONE (W)

FAX

CELL/PAGER

NAME

ADDRESS

EMAIL

PHONE (H)

PHONE (W)

FAX

CELL/PAGER

NAME

ADDRESS

EMAIL

PHONE (H)

PHONE (W)

FAX

CELL/PAGER

NAME

ADDRESS

EMAIL

PHONE (H)

PHONE (W)

FAX

CELL/PAGER

NAME

ADDRESS

EMAIL

PHONE (H)

PHONE (W)

FAX

CELL/PAGER

NAME

ADDRESS

EMAIL

PHONE (H)

PHONE (W)

FAX

CELL/PAGER

Kavavaow Mannomee
Grey Owl, 1993
Stonecut and stencil, 76.2 x 62.1 cm (30 x 24⁷⁄₁₆ in.)
Printer: Kavavaow Mannomee

T

Kenojuak Ashevak
Siilavut, Nunavut, 1999
Lithograph diptych, 113 x 76 cm overall (44^{7}⁄₁₆ x 29^{15}⁄₁₆ in.)
Printer: Pitseolak Niviaqsi

NAME _____ PHONE (H) _____

ADDRESS _____ PHONE (W) _____

_____ FAX _____

EMAIL _____ CELL/PAGER _____

NAME _____ PHONE (H) _____

ADDRESS _____ PHONE (W) _____

_____ FAX _____

EMAIL _____ CELL/PAGER _____

NAME _____ PHONE (H) _____

ADDRESS _____ PHONE (W) _____

_____ FAX _____

EMAIL _____ CELL/PAGER _____

NAME _____ PHONE (H) _____

ADDRESS _____ PHONE (W) _____

_____ FAX _____

EMAIL _____ CELL/PAGER _____

NAME _____ PHONE (H) _____

ADDRESS _____ PHONE (W) _____

_____ FAX _____

EMAIL _____ CELL/PAGER _____

NAME _____ PHONE (H) _____

ADDRESS _____ PHONE (W) _____

_____ FAX _____

EMAIL _____ CELL/PAGER _____

NAME	PHONE (H)
ADDRESS	PHONE (W)
	FAX
EMAIL	CELL/PAGER

NAME	PHONE (H)
ADDRESS	PHONE (W)
	FAX
EMAIL	CELL/PAGER

NAME	PHONE (H)
ADDRESS	PHONE (W)
	FAX
EMAIL	CELL/PAGER

NAME	PHONE (H)
ADDRESS	PHONE (W)
	FAX
EMAIL	CELL/PAGER

NAME	PHONE (H)
ADDRESS	PHONE (W)
	FAX
EMAIL	CELL/PAGER

NAME	PHONE (H)
ADDRESS	PHONE (W)
	FAX
EMAIL	CELL/PAGER

NAME

ADDRESS

EMAIL

PHONE (H)

PHONE (W)

FAX

CELL/PAGER

NAME

ADDRESS

EMAIL

PHONE (H)

PHONE (W)

FAX

CELL/PAGER

NAME

ADDRESS

EMAIL

PHONE (H)

PHONE (W)

FAX

CELL/PAGER

NAME

ADDRESS

EMAIL

PHONE (H)

PHONE (W)

FAX

CELL/PAGER

NAME

ADDRESS

EMAIL

PHONE (H)

PHONE (W)

FAX

CELL/PAGER

NAME

ADDRESS

EMAIL

PHONE (H)

PHONE (W)

FAX

CELL/PAGER

NAME	PHONE (H)
ADDRESS	PHONE (W)
	FAX
EMAIL	CELL/PAGER

NAME	PHONE (H)
ADDRESS	PHONE (W)
	FAX
EMAIL	CELL/PAGER

NAME	PHONE (H)
ADDRESS	PHONE (W)
	FAX
EMAIL	CELL/PAGER

NAME	PHONE (H)
ADDRESS	PHONE (W)
	FAX
EMAIL	CELL/PAGER

NAME	PHONE (H)
ADDRESS	PHONE (W)
	FAX
EMAIL	CELL/PAGER

NAME	PHONE (H)
ADDRESS	PHONE (W)
	FAX
EMAIL	CELL/PAGER

Kavavaow Mannomee
Spring Caribou, 1995
Etching and aquatint, 60 x 68.9 cm (23⅝ x 27⅛ in.)
Printer: Studio PM

UV

Pitseolak Ashoona
Stepping Stones, 1983
Stonecut and stencil, 47.5 x 69 cm (18¾ x 27³⁄₁₆ in.)
Printer: Kooyoo Simiga

NAME

ADDRESS

EMAIL

PHONE (H)

PHONE (W)

FAX

CELL/PAGER

NAME

ADDRESS

EMAIL

PHONE (H)

PHONE (W)

FAX

CELL/PAGER

NAME

ADDRESS

EMAIL

PHONE (H)

PHONE (W)

FAX

CELL/PAGER

NAME

ADDRESS

EMAIL

PHONE (H)

PHONE (W)

FAX

CELL/PAGER

NAME

ADDRESS

EMAIL

PHONE (H)

PHONE (W)

FAX

CELL/PAGER

NAME

ADDRESS

EMAIL

PHONE (H)

PHONE (W)

FAX

CELL/PAGER

NAME

ADDRESS

EMAIL

PHONE (H)

PHONE (W)

FAX

CELL/PAGER

NAME

ADDRESS

EMAIL

PHONE (H)

PHONE (W)

FAX

CELL/PAGER

NAME

ADDRESS

EMAIL

PHONE (H)

PHONE (W)

FAX

CELL/PAGER

NAME

ADDRESS

EMAIL

PHONE (H)

PHONE (W)

FAX

CELL/PAGER

NAME

ADDRESS

EMAIL

PHONE (H)

PHONE (W)

FAX

CELL/PAGER

NAME

ADDRESS

EMAIL

PHONE (H)

PHONE (W)

FAX

CELL/PAGER

NAME	PHONE (H)
ADDRESS	PHONE (W)
	FAX
EMAIL	CELL/PAGER

NAME	PHONE (H)
ADDRESS	PHONE (W)
	FAX
EMAIL	CELL/PAGER

NAME	PHONE (H)
ADDRESS	PHONE (W)
	FAX
EMAIL	CELL/PAGER

NAME	PHONE (H)
ADDRESS	PHONE (W)
	FAX
EMAIL	CELL/PAGER

NAME	PHONE (H)
ADDRESS	PHONE (W)
	FAX
EMAIL	CELL/PAGER

NAME	PHONE (H)
ADDRESS	PHONE (W)
	FAX
EMAIL	CELL/PAGER

NAME

ADDRESS

EMAIL

PHONE (H)

PHONE (W)

FAX

CELL/PAGER

NAME

ADDRESS

EMAIL

PHONE (H)

PHONE (W)

FAX

CELL/PAGER

NAME

ADDRESS

EMAIL

PHONE (H)

PHONE (W)

FAX

CELL/PAGER

NAME

ADDRESS

EMAIL

PHONE (H)

PHONE (W)

FAX

CELL/PAGER

NAME

ADDRESS

EMAIL

PHONE (H)

PHONE (W)

FAX

CELL/PAGER

NAME

ADDRESS

EMAIL

PHONE (H)

PHONE (W)

FAX

CELL/PAGER

Lucy Qinnuayuak
Large Bear, 1961
Stonecut, 61 x 94 cm (24 x 37 in.)
Printer: Eegyvadluk Pootoogook

W

Sheojuk Etidlooie
Winter Bear, 1996
Etching and aquatint, 50 x 60 cm (19^{11}/$_{16}$ x 23^{5}/$_{8}$ in.)
Printer: Studio PM

NAME	PHONE (H)
ADDRESS	PHONE (W)
	FAX
EMAIL	CELL/PAGER

NAME	PHONE (H)
ADDRESS	PHONE (W)
	FAX
EMAIL	CELL/PAGER

NAME	PHONE (H)
ADDRESS	PHONE (W)
	FAX
EMAIL	CELL/PAGER

NAME	PHONE (H)
ADDRESS	PHONE (W)
	FAX
EMAIL	CELL/PAGER

NAME	PHONE (H)
ADDRESS	PHONE (W)
	FAX
EMAIL	CELL/PAGER

NAME	PHONE (H)
ADDRESS	PHONE (W)
	FAX
EMAIL	CELL/PAGER

NAME

ADDRESS

EMAIL

PHONE (H)

PHONE (W)

FAX

CELL/PAGER

NAME

ADDRESS

EMAIL

PHONE (H)

PHONE (W)

FAX

CELL/PAGER

NAME

ADDRESS

EMAIL

PHONE (H)

PHONE (W)

FAX

CELL/PAGER

NAME

ADDRESS

EMAIL

PHONE (H)

PHONE (W)

FAX

CELL/PAGER

NAME

ADDRESS

EMAIL

PHONE (H)

PHONE (W)

FAX

CELL/PAGER

NAME

ADDRESS

EMAIL

PHONE (H)

PHONE (W)

FAX

CELL/PAGER

NAME

PHONE (H)

ADDRESS

PHONE (W)

FAX

EMAIL

CELL/PAGER

NAME

PHONE (H)

ADDRESS

PHONE (W)

FAX

EMAIL

CELL/PAGER

NAME

PHONE (H)

ADDRESS

PHONE (W)

FAX

EMAIL

CELL/PAGER

NAME

PHONE (H)

ADDRESS

PHONE (W)

FAX

EMAIL

CELL/PAGER

NAME

PHONE (H)

ADDRESS

PHONE (W)

FAX

EMAIL

CELL/PAGER

NAME

PHONE (H)

ADDRESS

PHONE (W)

FAX

EMAIL

CELL/PAGER

NAME

ADDRESS

EMAIL

PHONE (H)

PHONE (W)

FAX

CELL/PAGER

NAME

ADDRESS

EMAIL

PHONE (H)

PHONE (W)

FAX

CELL/PAGER

NAME

ADDRESS

EMAIL

PHONE (H)

PHONE (W)

FAX

CELL/PAGER

NAME

ADDRESS

EMAIL

PHONE (H)

PHONE (W)

FAX

CELL/PAGER

NAME

ADDRESS

EMAIL

PHONE (H)

PHONE (W)

FAX

CELL/PAGER

NAME

ADDRESS

EMAIL

PHONE (H)

PHONE (W)

FAX

CELL/PAGER

Innukjuakju
Twilight Owl, 1962
Stonecut, 47 x 32 cm (18½ x 12⅝ in.)
Printer: Timothy Ottochie

Kenojuak Ashevak
Owl in Blue, 1991
Lithograph, 71.4 x 96.2 cm (28⅛ x 37⅞ in.)
Printer: Pitseolak Niviaqsi

NAME

ADDRESS

EMAIL

PHONE (H)

PHONE (W)

FAX

CELL/PAGER

NAME

ADDRESS

EMAIL

PHONE (H)

PHONE (W)

FAX

CELL/PAGER

NAME

ADDRESS

EMAIL

PHONE (H)

PHONE (W)

FAX

CELL/PAGER

NAME

ADDRESS

EMAIL

PHONE (H)

PHONE (W)

FAX

CELL/PAGER

NAME

ADDRESS

EMAIL

PHONE (H)

PHONE (W)

FAX

CELL/PAGER

NAME

ADDRESS

EMAIL

PHONE (H)

PHONE (W)

FAX

CELL/PAGER

NAME _____ PHONE (H) _____

ADDRESS _____ PHONE (W) _____

_____ FAX _____

EMAIL _____ CELL/PAGER _____

NAME _____ PHONE (H) _____

ADDRESS _____ PHONE (W) _____

_____ FAX _____

EMAIL _____ CELL/PAGER _____

NAME _____ PHONE (H) _____

ADDRESS _____ PHONE (W) _____

_____ FAX _____

EMAIL _____ CELL/PAGER _____

NAME _____ PHONE (H) _____

ADDRESS _____ PHONE (W) _____

_____ FAX _____

EMAIL _____ CELL/PAGER _____

NAME _____ PHONE (H) _____

ADDRESS _____ PHONE (W) _____

_____ FAX _____

EMAIL _____ CELL/PAGER _____

NAME _____ PHONE (H) _____

ADDRESS _____ PHONE (W) _____

_____ FAX _____

EMAIL _____ CELL/PAGER _____

NAME

ADDRESS

EMAIL

PHONE (H)

PHONE (W)

FAX

CELL/PAGER

NAME

ADDRESS

EMAIL

PHONE (H)

PHONE (W)

FAX

CELL/PAGER

NAME

ADDRESS

EMAIL

PHONE (H)

PHONE (W)

FAX

CELL/PAGER

NAME

ADDRESS

EMAIL

PHONE (H)

PHONE (W)

FAX

CELL/PAGER

NAME

ADDRESS

EMAIL

PHONE (H)

PHONE (W)

FAX

CELL/PAGER

NAME

ADDRESS

EMAIL

PHONE (H)

PHONE (W)

FAX

CELL/PAGER

NAME

ADDRESS

EMAIL

PHONE (H)

PHONE (W)

FAX

CELL/PAGER

NAME

ADDRESS

EMAIL

PHONE (H)

PHONE (W)

FAX

CELL/PAGER

NAME

ADDRESS

EMAIL

PHONE (H)

PHONE (W)

FAX

CELL/PAGER

NAME

ADDRESS

EMAIL

PHONE (H)

PHONE (W)

FAX

CELL/PAGER

NAME

ADDRESS

EMAIL

PHONE (H)

PHONE (W)

FAX

CELL/PAGER

NAME

ADDRESS

EMAIL

PHONE (H)

PHONE (W)

FAX

CELL/PAGER